❧ *To* ❧

❧ *From* ❧

101 Quick Tips
To Make Your Home
❧ FEEL ❧
SenseSational

Books by Terry Willits

101 Quick Tips to Make Your Home
Feel SenseSational

101 Quick Tips to Make Your Home
Look SenseSational

101 Quick Tips to Make Your Home
Smell SenseSational

101 Quick Tips to Make Your Home
Sound SenseSational

101 Quick Tips to Make Your Home
Taste SenseSational

Creating a SenseSational Home

If you are interested in having Terry Willits speak to your
church, organization, or special event, please contact:

InterAct Speaker's Bureau
8012 Brooks Chapel Road, Suite 243
Brentwood, Tennessee 37027
Telephone (800) 370-9932
Fax (615) 370-9939

101 Quick Tips
To Make Your Home
❧ FEEL ❧
SenseSational

TERRY WILLITS

ZondervanPublishingHouse
Grand Rapids, Michigan

A Division of HarperCollins*Publishers*

101 Quick Tips to Make Your Home Feel SenseSational
Copyright © 1996 by Terry Willits

Requests for information should be addressed to:

🏭 ZondervanPublishingHouse
Grand Rapids, Michigan 49530

Library of Congress Cataloging-in-Publication Data

Willits, Terry, 1959–
    101 quick tips to make your home feel SenseSational / Terry Willits.
        p.   cm.
    ISBN: 0-310-20228-0
    1. House furnishings.   2. Interior decoration.   3. Touch.   4. Christian life.
    I. Title.
TX311.W535   1996
645—dc20

                                                                        96-13327
                                                                        CIP

This edition printed on acid-free paper and meets the American National Standards Institute Z39.48 standard.

All Scripture quotations, unless otherwise indicated, are taken from the *Holy Bible: New International Version*®. NIV®. Copyright © 1973, 1978, 1984 by International Bible Society. Used by permission of Zondervan Publishing House. All rights reserved.

Edited by Rachel Boers
Interior Illustrations by Edsel Arnold
Interior design by Sherri L. Hoffman

Printed in the United States of America

96 97 98 99 00 01 02 /❖ QF/ 10 9 8 7 6 5 4 3 2 1

The wise woman builds her house, but with her own hands the foolish one tears hers down.

Proverbs 14:1

Introduction

— ⚜ —

*T*ouch is the sense at the deepest root of our emotions. It is unlike any other sense in that it can be stimulated by every inch of the body — God has covered our bodies with approximately five million receptors to experience touch.

This powerful, yet delicate sense affects nearly everything we do in our homes. We touch people. We touch things. Every touch can bring a blessing to where we live, whether it be a gentle kiss, a warm hug, a tender stroke, a comfortable chair, a hot bath, or a cozy quilt. Unfortunately, the busier our lives become, the less time we take to enjoy touch.

May the following tips inspire you to slow down enough to enjoy the comforting touches that already fill your home, and motivate you to discover new touches as well. A simple touch can mean so much. Treasure God's gift of touch in your home.

terry.

101 Quick Tips
To Make Your Home
❧ FEEL ❧
SenseSational

1

Get in touch with touch.

*A*waken your sense of touch in the home you create. Notice the feel of fabrics and furnishings as you touch them. Use the hands God has given you not just for laboring, but for loving. Make every effort to fill your home with loving touches of comfort.

2

Make the first step satisfying.

*G*reet guests with a pretty area rug inside your front door. It will be their first touch of comfort as they step into your home. Select a rug with a background color or busy pattern  that will camouflage dirt. For comfort, and to prevent slipping, place a vinyl mesh grip beneath it. For extra cushion, use a piece of carpet padding in place of the mesh grip.

Give homecoming hugs and kisses.

$\mathcal{A}$ cheerful homecoming shows love, respect, and admiration. Try to be home to welcome family at the end of their day. Stop whatever you're doing and greet them at the door with a warm hug or kiss.

4

Welcome visitors warmly.

*G*reet visitors to your home with a warm hug or firm handshake. For an extra touch of sincerity, give a double-handed handshake. Such thoughtful gestures of touch instantly convey love and acceptance and put others at ease in your home.

Please sign on the line.

*D*isplay a beautiful guest book and a pen on a table by your front door. Invite visitors to sign it as they leave your home. This little book will soon hold cherished memories of special times spent with friends and family in your home.

6

Beautify with blankets.

Collect mohair, cotton, or wool blankets in pretty patterns, textures, and colors. Beautiful throws and blankets add texture, charm, and security wherever they are. Use them throughout your home — draped over a sofa or chair, folded at the end of a bed, or stacked on a bench. Keep them within easy reach for a touch of cozy comfort.

Cozy up to a quilt.

*O*ld or new, quilts are a lovely and long-lasting way to bring the color and comfort of cotton to your home year-round. Collect pretty quilts that coordinate with your decor. Use them as bed coverlets or wall hangings, fold and stack them on top of a chest, or drape one over a table and cover it with glass.

8

Roll out the rugs.

Colorful cotton rag or braided rugs soften a hard, cold floor. These rugs are comfortable, reasonably priced, and reversible. Scatter small ones in places where you stand frequently — in front of your shower, tub, or kitchen sink, and at front and back doors. Do not use rag rugs on top of carpet where they might get wet and stain the carpet. For best results, dry clean.

Frame your furniture.

*U*se a large dhurrie, needlepoint, or Oriental area rug to frame a cozy seated area for conversation. Lay the rug either on a hard floor surface or on top of your carpet. To cushion the rug and prevent it from slipping, place a vinyl underlay or piece of carpet padding beneath it.

10

Step on it.

When selecting carpet, think quality first, then color. Walk on it with your bare feet to be sure it is soft. For high traffic areas, choose a durable, dense pile, tight level loop or cut-and-loop carpet. Use deeper, plush piles for lower traffic areas. Buy the best padding you can afford. The quality of the padding affects the comfort and life of your carpet.

Make furniture arrangements friendly.

*C*luster furniture comfortably together for conversation. Arrange pieces as if they were speaking to one another. Much like body language, furnishings placed in close proximity produce warmth, intimacy, and emotional connection among the people in the room.

If you have a large room, consider creating two smaller sitting areas.

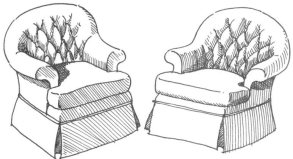

12

Splurge on a sofa.

A well-made, comfortable sofa will provide years of satisfying seating. Before buying a sofa, sit in it to make sure it's a fit. Seat height and depth, arm height, and cushion construction all contribute to a sofa's comfort. Though soft cushions may be more comfortable, firmer cushions will retain their shape better.

Pick a personal perch.

*P*lace a favorite, comfortable chair that suits your personality and your touch by a sunny window. It may be an overstuffed club chair, a wooden gliding rocker, or a chaise lounge. In a moment of stillness, steal away to your favorite seat to spend time alone with God.

14

Be flexible.

*F*or greater flexibility and enjoyment, consider adding casters or a swivel base to a new or reupholstered club chair. Both features will give you the freedom to swing one way to watch a roaring fire or twirl around to take part in a conversation. The slight additional cost will be well worth the added comfort and convenience.

15

Put your feet up.

Have an ottoman to raise weary legs anywhere in your home. Place it on casters to allow for the flexibility of additional seating. A large ottoman can be multifunctional — use it to prop feet up, to stack with beautiful books, or to accommodate a tray for serving food and beverages. An ottoman should be at least one inch lower than seat height of sofa or chair.

16

Keep it convenient.

*T*ry to have some type of table within reach of every seating piece in your home. This will provide a comfortable place to set a beverage, spool of thread, book, magazine, or whatever you need to keep close at hand.

Feel your fabrics.

*W*hen selecting fabrics, choose them for their feel as well as their look. Textured fabrics such as nubby wool, soft suede, woven linen, cool cotton, elegant damask, slippery chintz, or luscious velvet add interest and a pleasant touch to any upholstered furniture. The more textured and heavy a fabric, the more durable it is apt to be.

18

Go naturelle!

For a casual look, use natural fibers like sisal or sea grass rugs. With their neutral-colored, textured weave, these practical rugs subtly enhance any room that has hard surface flooring. Before buying, walk on rugs in your bare feet — some are more comfortable than others. For color, use a contrast binding on the edge of a rug or stencil a pattern.

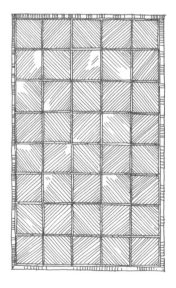

Toss in a touch of texture.

$\mathcal{C}$ollect pretty needlepoint pillows and toss one in with a mixture of other pillows on a sofa, chair, bed, or bench. Pull out a few Christmas needlepoint pillows every year around the holidays to help decorate your home.

20

Have happy hands.

*I*f you enjoy cross-stitching, knitting, or needlepoint, or simply need to stitch on a button now and then, a pretty sewing basket will make the job a joy. Fill your sewing basket with thread, yarn, needles, pins, sharp scissors, and a thimble. Keep it close at hand for whenever you have the itch to sit and work with your hands.

Find natural finishes.

*F*or an extra touch of charm and warmth, bring God's beauty into you home by using a variety of natural finishes. Consider wicker, wood, marble, stone, slate, brick, or granite.

Pile on the pillows.

Soft, squishy throw pillows come in many sizes and shapes, but all lend a touch of comfort to any corner of your home. Back beds, benches, sofas, or chairs with plump pillows. For extra-cushy comfort, use pillows filled with down — the comfortable filling will conform to your body for a cozy, satisfying backrest.

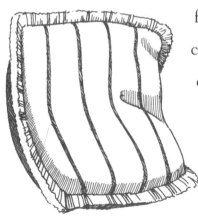

Plop onto floor pillows.

*K*eep two or three jumbo pillows stacked on the floor in your living room, playroom, or children's bedroom. They provide flexible seating and serve as a great support for someone who wants to sit on the floor to watch a movie or lounge in front of a roaring fire. Floor pillows are inexpensive compared to other seating, and with zippered coverings, they can be easily cleaned.

24

Texturize your home.

*F*ill your home with a variety of textured elements, such as an iron drapery rod, a woven wicker chair, or a carved clay sculpture. Bring texture and interest to damaged or ordinary walls by mixing sand with paint.

Enjoy the feel of a fan.

*I*nstall a ceiling fan to bring a breeze to any room. Use the small switch on your fan's axis to turn blades clockwise to stay cool in warm weather and counterclockwise to circulate heat in cold weather. A ceiling fan is more attractive and safer than most portable fans. Installing an attic fan will help circulate air in a two-story home.

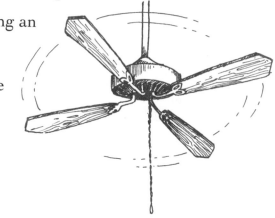

26

Own a cuddly companion.

*A*dopt a dog, cat, or other cuddly animal that likes to be held. The loving touch you give your pet will bring both of you loads of pleasure. If you live alone, a pet makes a comforting companion.

Don't make dusting a drag.

*T*hrow out those skimpy scraps of old T-shirts and tattered towels for dusting. Instead, buy a dozen cotton fabric diapers for dusting. Store them in a pretty basket, and wash them after each use. Use an ostrich feather duster with a long handle for hard-to-reach places. Make time spent dusting a time to thank God for all his blessings.

28

Open up.

*B*ring the wonderful feel of the outdoors inside by opening your windows on a pleasant day and enjoying the fresh, soothing breeze as it flows through your home and touches your skin.

Polish with pleasure.

$\mathscr{E}$njoy the act of polishing brass, glass, silver, or wood. Rubbing favorite objects and restoring their natural beauty can give a great sense of satisfaction.

30

Unveil your mail.

$\mathcal{M}$ake opening your mail a pleasant ritual with a pretty letter opener. Not only will it add beauty to the task, it will spare your hands and nails.

Make paperwork pretty.

*F*ind a lovely way to display paperwork that

needs your attention. Use a brass letter rack,

silver toast caddy, or basket for filing bills

and correspondence and responding

to invitations. Keeping invita-

tions will remind you to

write a thank-you note

as soon as you have

attended an event.

32

File with finesse.

$\mathcal{M}$ake your file system a pleasant place of
touch by organizing it efficiently. For easy
reference, color coordinate your file folders
according to different topics: personal,
business,
household, et cetera.

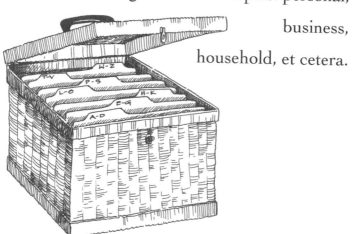

33

Write away.

*F*ill a pretty, compartmented basket with your favorite stationery, note cards, postcards, stamps, updated address book, labels, and a nice pen. The more convenient writing is, the more likely you are to keep in touch. Minister to others from your home through the mail.

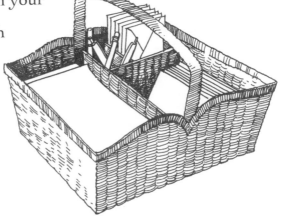

34

Strike one!

Make a hobby of collecting matches from restaurants, hotels, and other places you visit; you'll bring back memories every time you use one. Keep matchbooks in a convenient spot (out of reach of little ones) so they're handy when you need one. In the winter, keep tall wood matches in a wood box on your fireplace mantle. Or try a flame igniter, available in most hardware stores. It lights with an easy flick of the finger.

Tickle your tongue.

What type of ice do you prefer in cold beverages: crushed, small cubes, or large cubes? If you don't have an ice maker that produces your favorite ice, buy trays that will make them or purchase bags of the ice you prefer and store them in the freezer.

36

Buy the best.

*D*on't skimp on the quality of paper towels, toilet tissue, or facial tissue you use in your home. Find a brand you love for its touch, and stick with it. The better quality the paper

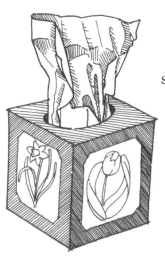

product, the less you will need. Use coupons, and stock up when your paper items go on sale. By purchasing extra-large rolls, you will save time and energy replacing them.

Open with ease.

*C*an opening need not be a chore. Have a quality manual or electric can opener that is dependable and works with ease. If you prefer electric, try an under-the-counter model to save on counter-top clutter.

38

Keep it cozy.

Use a tea cozy or tea towel around your teapot to keep your beverage warm. Transfer freshly brewed coffee to an airtight thermal carafe to keep it hot for several hours.

Grab your garbage.

*L*ine a large decorative trash can in your kitchen with a sturdy garbage bag that holds well and has a built-in drawstring. For a quick trick, store additional plastic bags in the bottom of your trash can. No more fumbling to find those ties, twisties, or replace-ment bags.

40

Take a number.

$\mathcal{K}$eep a handy basket next to the kitchen
telephone with a pen and notepad to jot down
messages and reminders. Use the spot for
your home's communication center. Always
leave a note if you must leave home before
someone else is expected to arrive; it's
courteous, thoughtful, and will give a sense
of security to anyone
entering an empty
home.

Add just a pinch.

*K*eep a small dish of salt by your stove in the kitchen. When your food needs a touch of salt, use your fingers to add just a pinch. Using your fingers will allow you to have greater control over the amount of salt used while cooking or preparing food than you would if using a salt shaker.

42

Keep it crispy.

Wrap chips, cereals, and crackers well to prevent moisture from causing them to go stale. Use clothespins, large paper clips, or plastic clips to secure folded bags. Or store crispy foods in your pantry in clear plastic containers.

Soften your spread.

$\mathcal{S}$preading a hard chuck of butter on a piece of warm toast or fresh bread can be one of life's little hang-ups. To keep it soft and spreadable, leave butter or margarine out on the counter or kitchen table in a covered butter dish.

44

Keep your touch tender.

*W*earing rubber gloves can spare your hands while washing dishes, or when opening tight lids on glass jars. Apply hand lotion to your hands from a decorative dispenser by your kitchen sink. Massaging your hands with lotion can be a small reward of touch after kitchen cleanup.

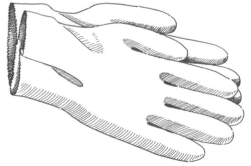

Cut it with a knife.

Sharpen knives and scissors when dull. A sharp tool makes cutting a pleasure and saves time. If you don't have a knife or scissors sharpener, many hardware stores offer professional sharpening. Protect your countertops by always cutting on a sturdy cutting board. Have a sharp pair of sewing scissors specially designated for cutting fabrics only.

46

Know your knives.

A large, wide chef's knife minces, chops, and slices fruits and vegetables. A narrower, long, slicing knife with a smooth-edged blade cuts thin, even slices of meats, vegetables, and cheeses. A serrated-edge saws breads and cakes. Use a paring knife for most small cutting jobs, and a medium-size utility knife to peel, slice, and chop.

Carve up a feast.

*H*ave an excellent carving knife and serving fork. For effortless carving, use a sharp electric knife. Carving a roast or turkey should be part of a celebration, not a frustration.

48

Collect spoons in all shapes and sizes.

*S*mooth wooden spoons make stirring, sautéing, or tossing food a delight. Collect a variety of them and store them in a decorative canister within easy reach of the stove.

Get a grip.

*T*ransform a door or cabinet by replacing its hardware with beautiful, functional knobs or handles that feel wonderful to your grasp.

50

Hold onto hot pots.

Treat yourself to a few new pot holders when
the old ones begin to look tired and tattered.
A fresh new set of holders will cost very little,
yet will add joy to your cooking
every time you put them on to
pick up something hot.

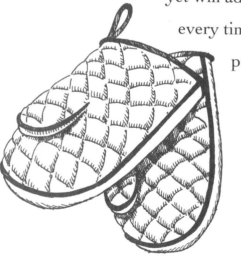

Make a splash
with dish towels.

*R*eplace kitchen dish towels when they become stained and dingy. Drape a pretty, all-cotton, absorbent dish towel over a kitchen cabinet door in front of your sink or thread one through your refrigerator door handle to wipe wet hands and dry dishes.

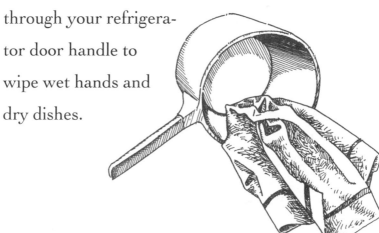

52

Tie your apron strings.

A pretty apron will add pleasure to a mundane chore, helping you prepare your heart and mind for your task, and changing what might be considered a burden into a blessing.

For a touch of casual comfort, hang a few aprons that coordinate with your kitchen colors on the pegs of a Shaker rack and place the rack in a prominent spot in your kitchen.

53

Create a window of opportunity.

*F*or comfort and coziness, transform a beautiful bay window into a functional window seat. Add hinges to the lid of your window seat to allow you to use the space below for storage. Make a seat cushion and pile on the pillows to make it a favorite perch for reading, eating, or just daydreaming.

54

Reach out and touch.

*H*old hands while praying at mealtime or any time. Give hands an extra "I love you" squeeze at the end of the prayer. The simple act of hand-holding can knit hearts and lives together.

Fold with a flair.

To enhance a pretty place setting, add some flair to your napkin folding. Use napkin rings, wired ribbon, raffia, clothespins, or a self-knotted bow. Thread a napkin through a teacup handle. Stuff a fluffy napkin in a stemmed glass. Buy a book on napkin folding and learn a few new, simple folds. Life is more fun when it's full of surprises!

56

Try terry cloth.

Small, fringed terry-cloth hand towels work great as informal, absorbent napkins. Keep a good supply on hand and use them every day. They're economical, easy to care for, comfortable to the touch, and great for messy finger foods.

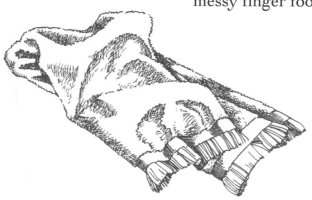

Help yourself.

*R*ather than set the table for a casual buffet with friends and family, let everyone help themselves from a utensil-holding basket caddy. Add creative flair by displaying silverware and napkin bundles in a decorative accessory like a ceramic vase or a teapot without a lid.

58

Clean up with class.

*P*rovide clean, dry hand towels and warm water with a slice of lemon, or rolled damp hand towels that have been heated in the microwave. After a messy meal of finger foods, serve them to your family and friends for a cleanup fit for royalty.

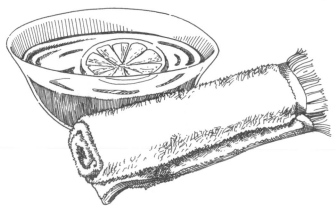

Bring a little luxury to your lips.

Using an appropriate glass for your beverage will enhance your touch and sipping satisfaction. Try a stemmed glass for fruit juice. A mason jar for iced tea. A chunky mug for coffee. A delicate cup for hot tea. Spoil those you love — as well as yourself — when serving a beverage by offering a small, pretty paper napkin or a coaster.

60

Turn on the temperature.

When it's hot, it's hot. When it's not, it's not. Complement the temperature of food items being served. Heat glass plates or bowls in a warm oven for hot foods. Chill plates, bowls, or glasses in the freezer for serving cold items.

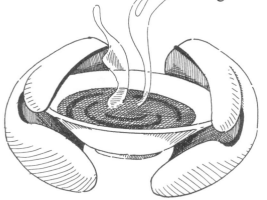

Soften your seat.

*B*uy or make pretty seat cushions for wood chairs. Add ties, tassels, or tufting to bring a little touch of beauty and comfort to seat cushions. To prevent chair pads from slipping and sliding when you sit on them, cut pieces of inexpensive vinyl rug grip and place them beneath the pad. Bring a touch of comfort to your bathroom with a cushioned toilet seat.

62

Protect with place mats.

Select place mats to protect your dining table that are both pretty and pleasing to the touch. Try natural woven mats for a casual look, or use easy-to-wipe-clean vinyl mats if you have children.

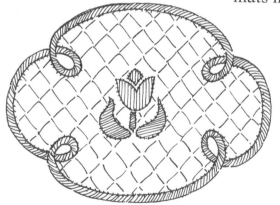

Robe yourself in comfort.

There's nothing more comfortable than wrapping yourself up in a plush terry cloth or cozy chenille bathrobe. Pick crisp, clean white or a color that looks pretty in your home. Keep your robe handy on a big hook behind your bathroom door.

64

Feel pretty as a princess.

$\mathcal{G}$et rid of old pajamas and keep just a few, pretty comfortable pieces of nightwear in fabrics like cotton, silk, flannel, rayon, or satin.

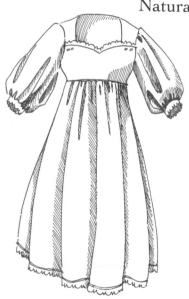

Natural fabrics allow your skin to breathe, providing a more comfortable, healthful sleep.

65

Hold on.

$\mathcal{A}$ hold is a hug that hangs on. Sometimes a warm embrace provides more help and healing than any wise advice or wonder drug. Try to sense when the situation calls for you to zip your lip and reach out your arms to hold a loved one.

66

Lounge around.

*P*itch the pitiful sweatpants and purchase at least one comfortable, attractive outfit that you can pull on when lounging around your home. You need not sacrifice beauty to be casual and comfortable. Of all places you should want to be attractive, it's in your private world with your loved ones.

Check it out.

*P*lace an outdoor thermometer outside your bedroom window. Check the temperature in the morning as you dress for the day.

68

Drape it.

*U*se a quilt rack as a caddy for coverlets, comforters, or bedspreads when they're not covering your bed. This will help keep them clean and fluffy and ensure they last longer.

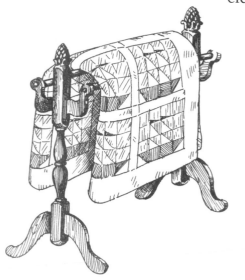

Up with down.

*I*nvest in a down duvet when they go on sale. A duvet is cool in the summer and warm in the winter and makes bed-making a breeze. With no top sheet or heavy blankets to wrestle, all you do is fluff and smooth! Place a duvet at the foot of a bed within reach for cozy comfort.

70

Get a good night's sleep.

*B*ecause we spend one-third of our lives in bed, a quality mattress is the wisest investment of material touch you can bring to your home. Flip your mattress every month to ensure it stays comfortable, wears better, and lasts longer. For maximum comfort and durability, purchase box springs and mattress as a set.

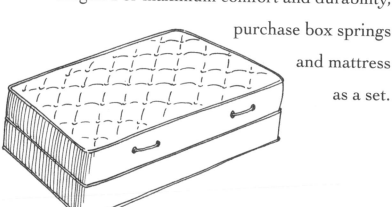

Cover up.

$\mathscr{P}$rotect mattresses and pillows with good quality covers. Buy mattress pads that fit well, and use a zippered pillow cover before slipping on a pillowcase. For a clean, tailored look, forego a bed skirt and cover your box springs with a fitted sheet to display a beautiful bed frame.

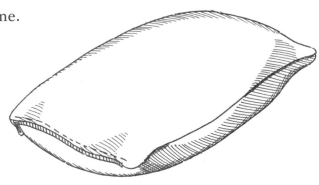

72

Satisfy with sheets.

Envelope your mattress in bedsheets that are beautiful, comfortable, and suitable to your personal preference for touch. Cool cotton sheets soothe in the summer. Cozy flannel sheets warm in the winter. Silky, satin sheets provide a little luxury anytime.

Find a cozy corner.

$\mathcal{D}$esignate a special spot in your home that is cozy, comfortable, and well-lighted as your place to be alone with God. The more convenient and comfortable it is, the more likely you will find yourself there. Keep your Bible, devotional book, and journal within easy reach.

74

Rest in peace.

*I*f time allows, and your body is craving it, take a short, guilt-free nap. There is a vast difference between laziness and rest. When you are weary, you need to rest. If you are overly tired, you'll become irritable and your perspective on life will become distorted. Refresh yourself and your outlook with adequate rest.

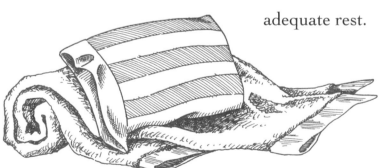

Pick a pillow.

*B*e picky about your bed pillows. Treat yourself to a favorite type and size, whether it be down, feathers, polyfill, or foam filling, king, queen, or standard size. Surround yourself with pillows that provide maximum comfort. Let each family member choose the pillow type he or she prefers.

76

Prop yourself with a pillow.

$\mathcal{U}$se a decorative pillow with arms and a firm back to prop you up while sitting in bed. Or, for lower back support, tuck a neck roll pillow behind several stacked bed pillows. A pillow prop will become a favorite item for reading, writing, or watching television in the privacy and comfort of your bedroom.

Touch a heart.

*F*or a touch of thoughtfulness, occasionally leave little sticky notes around your home for those you love. Put them where they're sure to be discovered — a mirror, phone receiver, bed pillow, or in a favorite shoe. It's a simple gesture that will touch their hearts, put a smile on their faces, and remind them they are loved.

78

Create a comfort zone.

*Y*our bedroom should be your most private comfort zone, a place to sit, read, and enjoy a morning cup of coffee or a midnight snack. If possible, create a small sitting area in your bedroom that includes a love seat or two chairs and a tea table. If space is tight, consider a chaise lounge and a small table.

Jot in a journal.

*K*eep in touch with your own personal thoughts and prayers by writing in a journal as often as you can; it helps clear your mind of clutter, allows you to see patterns in your life, and shows you God's faithful hand in unraveling life's challenges.

80

Scrub a dub dub.

*P*our liquid body soap onto a soft mesh puff and scrub all over your body. The bubbling lather and tingling touch will invigorate you!

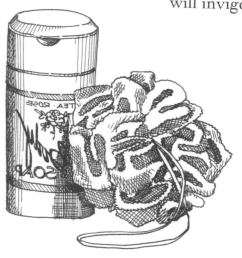

Touch toes.

*T*ake time to snuggle, cuddle, and touch toes with your mate or children. Make Saturday morning a time for everyone to pile in bed (pets too!) and get close.

82

Supply a soothing touch.

*K*eep your bathroom stocked with supplies for first aid and aches and pains. Be sure to have a heating pad, hot water bottle, and soothing ointment on hand. Bring comfort and loads of love to a loved one by giving a gentle rub to an aching limb, neck, or back. A small drop of baby oil will help your hands glide over weary muscles.

Save it for a rainy day.

*F*or an effortless way to save toward some-

thing special for your home, keep

a pretty jar on your bedroom

dresser to store loose

change from your purse or

pockets.

84

Keep closets clutter-free.

*M*ake putting on your clothes a pleasure by cleaning out your closet and drawers. Sort through your wardrobe every spring and fall. Lay all your clothes out on your bed, then try each garment on. If it fits and you wear it, keep it. If it needs mending or altering, fix it. If you haven't worn it in a year, give it away and allow someone else to enjoy it.

Keep current
addresses handy.

*T*o avoid having to replace an address book, use a decorative recipe file box. Write names and addresses of friends and relatives on individual index cards and file the cards alphabetically. When an address changes, simply pull the card and replace it with an updated one.

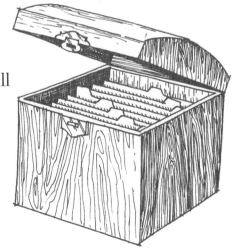

86

Bathe in bliss.

*D*raw up a warm bath for yourself or a loved one to soothe and relax before a good night's sleep. Add foaming bubble bath to tickle your body as you soak. Use a plastic bath air pillow to rest your head while soaking in the tub.

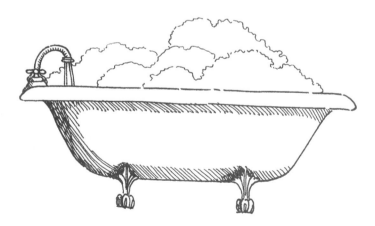

Collect touches for the tub.

*K*eep all of the necessary ingredients for a wonderful bath at your fingertips. Fill a basket next to the tub with your favorite soaps, bath salts, lotions, powders, sponges, and brushes.

88

Step safely.

Use plush, absorbent cotton rugs to soak up slippery splashes outside your shower or tub and keep your feet safe and comfortable. They are reversible, machine washable, and available in a rainbow of colors.

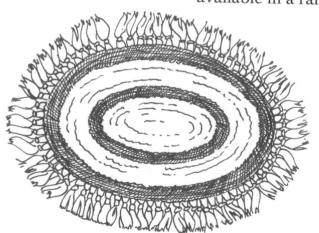

Pamper with a powder puff.

*A*pply a favorite perfumed powder all over your body with a big, fluffy duster. Use the powder puff on young children after a bath. They'll treasure its touch as it tickles their bodies from head to toe.

90

Store tiny touches.

*S*tore cotton swabs and soft, fluffy cotton balls in pretty decorative canisters on a bathroom shelf — they'll be close at hand for a tiny touch to clean your body. For a colorful touch, buy pastel cotton swabs and balls that coordinate with your bathroom decor.

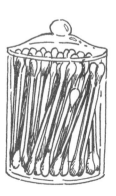

Have healthy hands.

*K*eep a decorative dispenser of liquid soap by every sink in your home to remind you and your family to wash your hands frequently. This simple habit can help keep your household healthy by preventing the spread of germs which lead to sickness.

92

Lather up.

*D*iscover a soap that you love, not just for its fragrance, but for its shape in your hand and the lather it makes. Enjoy the clean sensation as you lather your whole body in it. Rinse with warm water.

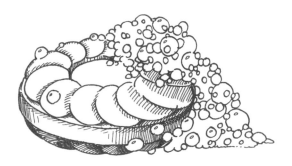

Baby your body.

*F*ind a face and body lotion that has a pleasing texture and soothes the skin. Display it in a decorative squirt dispenser, or store it out of sight when not in use. Apply frequently for a soft touch and a fresh, healthy glow. Treasure the time of touch as you care for your body. After all, it is God's temple!

94

Add a tingling touch.

*F*or a revitalizing tingle, add an adjustable
massage attachment to your showerhead.
Adjust the massage control to pulsate the
water pressure. The greater the water
pressure, the more invigorating
your shower will be.

Lighten your load.

Have separate laundry baskets for light and dark clothes to avoid having to sort later. Set aside specific times of the week to do laundry. This will help you work smarter, not harder, and will eliminate needless energy and stress. Pray as you fold laundry, thanking God for each loved one he's brought into your life.

96

Wrap yourself in love.

*R*oll up plush terry-cloth towels and put them in a pretty basket or stack them neatly on a small chair or wicker table by the tub. Fold or roll several small terry-cloth hand towels in a basket by the sink for drying hands and face. For a fresh-out-of-the-dryer feel, buy a towel-warming rack. After a shower or bath, wrap yourself in a big, warm, terry-cloth towel.

Weigh in.

$\mathcal{K}$eep an accurate scale in your bathroom or closet. Place it on a sturdy, solid surface when you weigh yourself. Maintaining a healthy body weight affects your attitude and energy level, both of which affect your home's atmosphere.

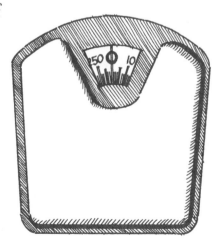

98

Dig in!

When planting flowers, vegetables, or greenery, put on a pair of gardening gloves and dig down deep into the dirt. Using your hands to nurture God's rich soil can be therapeutic. Proper soil preparation is essential for healthy growing plants, so mix nutrient-filled mulch into loose soil before planting.

Welcome with wonderful touches.

*H*elp overnight visitors feel at home with thoughtful touches of comfort like fresh towels, a bed of pretty linens, lots of plump pillows, and a cozy blanket or quilt.

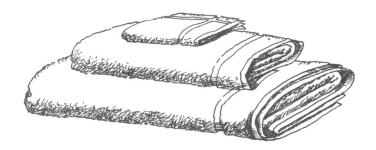

100

Secure your safety.

*F*or peace of mind, make sure you have sturdy locks on all windows and exterior doors. Ideally, all exterior doors should have dead-bolt locks. Keep a key to each dead bolt inside and close at hand, but not in the lock. Or, install a dead bolt that opens with the turn of a knob instead of a key.

101

Stay in touch with the Master.

Keep in touch with God by carving out quiet time in your day to spend reading your Bible, writing in a journal, and praying. Getting in touch with the heart of your heavenly Father will help you keep proper perspective on your life. As he brings balance to your day, gentle touches of love will no doubt be a part of the blessing you bring to your home.

More from Terry Willits . . .

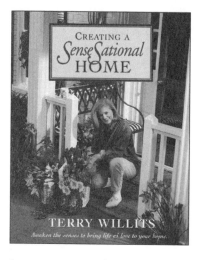

Creating a SenseSational Home is the complete guide to discover how awakening the five senses of sight, smell, taste, touch, and sound can create an atmosphere of love and cheer. From warmly-lit entrances that welcome family and friends to comfortable, homey interiors that invite them to stay and unwind . . . from fragrant bouquets to the tranquil ticking of a clock . . . *Creating a SenseSational Home* shows you simple and affordable ways to turn your home into a relaxing, inviting, and refreshing environment.

ISBN 0-310-20223-X
$19.99

ZondervanPublishingHouse

Grand Rapids, Michigan
http://www.zondervan.com

A Division of HarperCollins*Publishers*

America Online
AOL Keyword:zon